A section of the rich floor of Maw & Company tiles in the sanctuary of St Asaph Cathedral, Denbighshire. The tiles were put in during Sir Gilbert Scott's restoration of 1867–75.

Church Tiles of the Nineteenth Century

Kenneth Beaulah and Hans van Lemmen

Published in 2001 by Shire Publications Ltd,
Cromwell House, Church Street, Princes Risborough,
Buckinghamshire HP27 9AA, UK.
(Website: www.shirebooks.co.uk)

British Library Cataloguing in Publication Data:
Beaulah, G. K.
Church tiles of the nineteenth century. – 2nd ed. – (A Shire
album; 184)
I. Tiles – History – 19th century
I. Title II. Van Lemmen, Hans
738.6'09 ISBN 0 7478 0502 4

Front cover: *A panel of twenty-five 6 inch (152 mm) tiles from the reredos of Christ Church, Scarborough, North Yorkshire, demolished c.1980. Relief majolica by the Campbell Brick & Tile Company, c.1876. (Two tiles at the bottom, St Luke and St John, are missing. The spaces are filled by imagined figures.)*

Back cover: *An encaustic commemorative tile dedicated to Herbert Minton and installed, after his death in 1858, in the chancel of St Catherine, Barmby Moor, near Pocklington, East Yorkshire. Herbert Minton made two gifts of encaustic tiles to this church in 1849 and 1851.*

NOTE: Although tiles are referred to as 6 inch (152 mm) and 4 1/4 inch (108 mm) tiles, these were nominal sizes used by the manufacturers and may vary by as much as 1/8 inch (3 mm).

ACKNOWLEDGEMENTS
The following people and institutions have been of assistance in the production of this book: Dr R. W. Baker, George Baugh, Robert Copeland, Chris Cox, Richard Dennis, Betty Greene, Martin Hammond, Miranda Hankins, Wendy Harvey, Leslie Hayward, Tony Herbert, Sandy Heslop, Alyn Giles Jones, Joan Jones, Murdo Macdonald, Lynn Pearson, John Powell, John Rumsby, Margaret Sanders, Thelma Shepley, C. M. Simpson, Vincent Tyrell, Alexandra Wedgwood, A. M. Wherry, Julie Anne Wilson, the National Art Library and the National Museums and Galleries on Merseyside Archives Department, and the Tiles and Architectural Ceramics Society Ceramic Location Database.
All the photographs are from the collections of the authors.

Printed in Malta by Gutenberg Press Limited, Gudja Road,
Tarxien PLA 19, Malta.

Contents

Godwin tiles with a design of a Greek cross stretching over four tiles.

Minton & Company tiles in the sanctuary of St Giles's church, Cheadle, Staffordshire. The church was designed by A. W. N. Pugin for Lord Shrewsbury and was opened in 1846. The tiles, which are all designed by Pugin, are an integral element of the rich and colourful decorations of the whole interior.

Introduction

At the height of the Gothic Revival an insatiable demand for decorated floor tiles allowed makers to go to the best designers. Famous names in the field of ceramics manufactured tiles with inlaid designs (encaustic) for which awards were won at the principal international exhibitions. Their manufacture gave employment to thousands. In cathedrals – and even in small parish churches – one may see displays of ornamental tile paving notable for their energetic inventiveness, decorative qualities, religious symbolism and sound craftsmanship.

A. W. N. Pugin placed encaustic tiles 'near the head of those church ornaments which, next to stained glass, and when used in a wholehearted way, most charm the eye'. Certainly, when a new church was built, the local press or a periodical such as *The Builder* seldom failed to name the tiles among its beauties.

Yet church tiles of the nineteenth century have in our own day tended to be dismissed as machine-made products of little interest. Guide books almost never give them a mention. In part this may be due to the difficulty of identifying makers. The illustrations in manufacturers' catalogues have helped, but they are too small to recognise positively the work of different makers who may have copied the same medieval original. The tiles themselves, however, when placed side by side, can always be distinguished. The majority of loose tiles in collections are well marked on the backs and it is only necessary, usually, to recognise one tile in a pavement to attribute the whole. It is hoped that this, the first book on the subject, may help to further the reappraisal, which has already begun, of the decorative value and architectural interest of church tiles.

Medieval tiles and the Gothic Revival

For centuries after the Roman occupation the usual material for ground floors was nothing more than beaten earth. Stone or plaster was used in more important buildings and from about 1200 onwards glazed tiles were ordered only by rich abbeys or by the king himself. By 1300 two sorts of ornamental ceramic paving were well established. The first, and earlier, was composed of tiles cut in various shapes, glazed light or dark with lead oxide, in roughly equal numbers, fitted together in geometrical arrangements and relying on the colour contrasts between adjacent pieces for decorative effect. The other sort was formed almost entirely of square tiles, a proportion of them being decorated with designs either inlaid or indented, the ornamental effect of the floor being enhanced by grouping the decorated tiles in fours, nines or sixteens, with bands of plain tiles between. Byland Abbey in North Yorkshire is a prime example of the first sort, Cleeve Abbey, Somerset, of the second.

Contrast in colour in the early mosaic pavements was achieved by trowelling a thin surface layer of white-burning clay on the slabs of clay from which the light coloured tiles were to be cut. In effect this process was halfway to the inlaid decorated tile. For these a deep-cut wooden stamp was pressed on to a white-coated slab of clay while it was still plastic. Next the surface layer

An early thirteenth-century mosaic tile pavement at Byland Abbey, North Yorkshire. It features a circular pavement made up of different geometrically shaped tiles surrounded by areas of tile mosaic. It can clearly be seen how light and dark coloured tiles alternate to achieve interesting design effects.

Inlaid tiles at Cleeve Abbey, Somerset, with tiles showing fleur-de-lis motifs and designs with double-headed eagles, the device of Richard of Cornwall, brother of Henry III, as King of the Romans (1267–72).

was scraped away until the white clay remained only where the stamp had pressed it deeper than the surface of the clay body. According to the original thickness of the white layer, the lines of the pattern would be either narrow or broad, and it is this which is the cause of the great variation and uncertainty of outline so characteristic of the general run of medieval tiles. It was a misunderstanding of the medieval process by Victorian manufacturers such as Minton and others which was to be the cause of many complaints that their Gothic Revival tiles had an unpleasantly mechanical finish when compared with the medieval product. Some of the finest medieval tiles were made by stamping the plain clay, then filling the indentations with white clay.

Two thirteenth-century inlaid tiles at Winchester Cathedral depicting foliage combined with fleur-de-lis motifs and a heraldic lion in a circle. Such tiles served as inspiration for nineteenth-century manufacturers of encaustic tiles.

Part of a page from Parker's 'Glossary of Architecture', third edition, 1840. The first accurately drawn collection of medieval tiles to be published, it was used by early manufacturers for their exemplars.

From 1300 onwards, production of decorated tiles became a major industry. Whereas before tilers had tended to build their kilns close to each big tiling job, it now became usual for kilns to be located permanently where there was both clay and fuel and for tiles to be sent, mostly by water transport, to distant patrons. The devices used to decorate tiles in the medieval period were more numerous than those found on Victorian tiles: Victorian manufacturers were too sensitive about propriety and over-conscious that their tiles were destined for 'sacred edifices'. The old tilers depicted anything that came to mind, from acrobats to mermaids. As the industry neared its end, personalised tiles or groups of tiles became common, incorporating initials or the depiction of a name in the form of a graphic pun called a rebus. Heraldry always provided an endless source of decorative material.

Two-colour tiles in the form they had maintained for three centuries received their death blow from two quarters between 1537 and 1550. In 1537 the tilers lost their chief customers as the dissolution of the monasteries began, and polychrome faience (tin-glazed) tiles began to be imported from Antwerp at this time. Once these had been seen by wealthy patrons, the old two-colour inlaid tiles seemed hopelessly old-fashioned. A few tin-glazed tiles made by the 'cuenca' technique (in which the spaces

A thirteenth-century mosaic tile setting, approximately 7 feet (2.13 metres) square, formerly at Jervaulx Abbey, North Yorkshire. It was made up of 452 curvilinear inlaid tiles.

between raised lines of the design are filled with coloured enamel) were also entering Britain from Spain, and the mere knowledge that these existed seems to have postponed any plans for laying ornamental tile floors until Dutch polychrome tiles became available around 1580. After it became clear, however, that these painted tiles had only a short life under foot, hardly any decorated floor tiles were made in Britain until the 1830s, except for a small industry in North Devon, producing embossed and slip-decorated tiles, which ended soon after 1700.

Interest in the 'history and antiquities' of the medieval period grew rapidly in the second half of the eighteenth century. In the first half of the nineteenth century there was a great upsurge of religious observance and hundreds of new churches were needed, especially in towns, where population had often doubled in the wake of the Industrial Revolution. Before 1800 the few new churches built were in the Georgian or classical mode, but in the nineteenth century the Gothic style pervaded everything and by 1850 had become almost a national style, considered suitable for houses, town halls or railway stations: for churches, it was obligatory. The general prosperity, moreover, provided the funds for restoring or enlarging existing churches and reproductions of medieval tiles were as necessary as screens, lecterns, choir seating and many other church furnishings. Beautification of a chancel nearly always included the laying of an expanse of such tiles which became more elaborate as it reached the altar.

The young architect-designer Augustus Welby Northmore Pugin (1812–52), with vast energy and a fanatical interest in reviving medieval styles of building and ritual, became the apostle and chief propagator of an informed Gothic Revival movement. His opinions were widely accepted and his advice sought. Commissions poured into his office. Benjamin Ferrey, his friend and biographer, wrote that 'among the various objects occupying Pugin's attention, not one received a greater share than the revival of the manufacture of encaustic tiles'.

The inventor and his process

Samuel Wright (1783–1849), of Shelton, Staffordshire, patented his inlaying process for hard-wearing paving tiles in 1830. He had experience of making plain quarries and started manufacturing encaustic tiles. He was unlucky in aiming at the domestic rather than the ecclesiastical market and, becoming discouraged, sold his moulds and equipment in 1835 to Herbert Minton of the china works situated at Stoke little more than a mile from his own works. Wisely, however, he kept the patent rights and Minton used the process under licence. The only floor of Wright's tiles at present known is one at Kilmory Castle, Argyll, supplied by Minton out of the stock he had taken over. The tiles, laid about 1837, are of Moorish, not Gothic, design.

Wright's method, later perfected by Minton, was roughly as follows. The design was carved by hand into the flat surface of a block of plaster. The cavities were about 1/8 inch (3 mm) deep and flat-bottomed. Next, an open frame of cast iron was laid on the plaster (which had been brushed with soft soap to prevent sticking) and the frame was filled level with more plaster. After

Illustration in the 'Penny Magazine' of 1843 showing a tilemaker at work at Chamberlain's encaustic tile works. The screw press used for forcing the clay into the plaster moulds can be seen, while the workman is probably scraping excess white clay from a tile to reveal the inlaid design.

Workbench on show at the Gladstone Pottery Museum, Stoke-on-Trent, with a small screw press for the manufacture of encaustic tiles. On the back wall hang metal frames into which plaster moulds would be fitted when tiles were pressed. On the bench are wooden bats with spiked metal plates used for impressing holes into the backs of encaustic tiles.

separating, the plaster in its iron frame, with the design now in relief, became the working mould. The hand-carved master mould was kept in reserve for making new working moulds as they wore out. A second open frame, of the same size as the first and the depth of the finished tile, was laid upon the mould, located by pins engaging with holes in projecting lugs. The top open frame was then filled with plastic clay pushed into the corners by hand and left proud by an amount which experience told the operator would completely fill the mould when pressed. Any excess was squeezed out between press-plate and frame. (At Godwin's a piece of leather, presumably soaked in oil, was placed on the clay to prevent it sticking to the press-plate.) When the press-plate was raised and the pair of frames drawn forward the smooth clay back of the tile was then imprinted with the various factory marks described later. The upper clay-filled frame was then eased off the mould and turned over. The surface now showed the design deeply moulded in the dark-coloured body-clay. Pale-coloured clay the consistency of soft butter was trowelled across the tile and pressed down with the same movement (at Godwin's the slip clay was very fluid, poured from a jug). After the clay had stiffened a little,

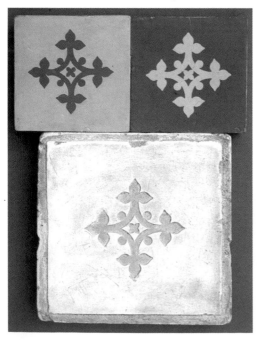

A nineteenth-century plaster master mould from the Minton, Hollins & Company factory with a design by A. W. N. Pugin. The two encaustic Minton tiles shown above show a similar motif.

The encaustic tilemaker Chris Cox pours white slip into the indented design of a fleur-de-lis. When the white slip is leather-hard it will be scraped level with the brown tile body.

a straight-edge of steel was drawn across. Resting on the frame, it evenly removed all superfluous slip, leaving the pattern clean against its darker background. After a day or so for drying and consequent shrinking, the tile could be easily pushed from its frame. After a more thorough drying the sides and back edges of the tile were pared by hand, ready for the kiln. If the tiles were to be glazed, a second firing was necessary. Minton and other makers devised a method, never fully described, by which plastic clay tiles were inlaid with two or three colours by making additional indentations after the first impression had been filled and scraped.

The powder-clay process (Prosser's) for making tiles, which could be described as the most productive innovation in the ceramics industry in the nineteenth century, was patented in 1840 and relied on pressing powdered clay, very slightly damped, into a metal mould from which it could be ejected immediately. No warping occurred and shrinkage was much less than with plastic clay. It was at once applied to the manufacture of white wall tiles, for which there came to be an immense demand, and was also adopted, though to a lesser extent, by makers of church tiles. Another invention (Boulton & Worthington's, 1863) made possible the dust-pressing of inlaid floor tiles with up to seven different colours.

In the interests of economy, all makers adopted a device which allowed the body of the tile to be of coarser clay, with finer clay at the surface. To avoid warping, this had to be balanced by a similar layer at the back. Tiles not needing a very smooth surface, such as those with a 'distressed' finish, were made of coarser clay throughout.

The manufacturers

CHAMBERLAIN OF WORCESTER

This firm was founded by Robert Chamberlain in 1786 and soon earned a high reputation for making fine porcelain. In 1836 Walter Chamberlain, of the third generation, was encouraged by his friend Harvey Eginton, a Worcester architect and antiquary, to take up the manufacture of inlaid tiles by Samuel Wright's

process. Eginton supplied some original designs as well as tracings from old examples. In sympathy with the rough finish of medieval work, Chamberlain did not strive after mechanical perfection and so was able to offer his tiles to church architects two or three years before Minton was ready.

In 1840 Chamberlain & Company amalgamated with Flight, Barr & Barr, an older porcelain manufacturer of Palace Row. The new company, trading under the same name, concentrated all porcelain production at Chamberlain's old works and, to make room for it, moved tilemaking over to Palace Row, where two partners, George Barr and Fleming St John, took over management and issued a first catalogue of seventy-seven tile designs in 1844.

Characteristic of Chamberlain's tiles is a high-gloss translucent yellow glaze which turns the red clay brown and the

Above: *Chamberlain tiles on the back wall of Great Malvern Priory, Worcestershire, c.1845. The patterned tiles are based on medieval examples.*

Right: *Chamberlain tiles on the floor of Slebech church, near Haverfordwest, Pembrokeshire. The plain tiles in the centre form a cross with a tile bearing the IHS monogram (the holy name of Jesus).*

white inlay yellow, muted in places by stain from the body clay. The slip was evidently sometimes poured in a very fluid state since it often ran down the sides of the tile. The mark, in two lines of type, is CHAMBERLAIN & CO WORCESTER. The front of the tile only has a facing of finer clay. Some tiles are slightly warped; others show cracks in the inlay. Only two colours (yellow and brown) are seen. Distribution is mainly confined to the Midlands, Wales and the south of England. The firm ceased to make tiles in 1848 and sold their equipment to J. H. Maw in 1850.

Chamberlain tiles.

13

Minton & Company tiles at Temple Church, London, showing the Holy Lamb, which was the emblem of the Inns of Court (Middle Temple), 1841–2.

MINTON OF STOKE-ON-TRENT

'The history of Minton's tilemaking is the history of the nineteenth-century industry', to paraphrase the ceramic historian Llewellyn Jewitt, who followed it by a picturesque account of a five-year struggle by Herbert Minton to achieve successful results. By 1841 Minton was confident enough to accept a big commission for a new pavement of inlaid tiles for the Temple Church, London, then being restored. The designs were mainly from tracings of twenty-four medieval patterns on tiles uncovered in the same year in the chapter house of Westminster Abbey. The work was successfully completed and enormously impressed church architects and an astonished public. This floor was badly damaged during the Second World War and a new one of stone was substituted. Fortunately much of the tile pavement was saved and re-laid in the gallery over the rotunda

A range of different Minton & Company tiles on the floor of York Minster chapter house, c.1845. The inlaid designs have been painted over with yellow enamel glaze.

Minton & Company tiles at St Mary's, Shrewsbury, c.1845. The tiles with lionesses on the left are based on the medieval tiles at Westminster Abbey chapter house.

arcade, where it may be seen on application to the verger.

One critic said that Chamberlain's early floors looked like linoleum. Minton avoided that by not glazing the body of his tiles at all, merely painting over the inlaid parts with yellow vitreous enamel. Tiles could also be ordered entirely unglazed, which was the preferred finish until about 1880, when an all-glazed surface came to be increasingly demanded, probably because of pressure from church cleaners. Minton modified a too bright surface by random indentations and by darkening the inlay, giving to their late tiles a fairly authentic medieval look. A Minton innovation was the use of blue or white 'jasper' clay as an inlay material. This is seen mainly between about 1844 and 1865. A black body instead of the red was sometimes used from 1842 to about 1875.

Minton & Company tiles designed by A. W. N. Pugin, which were donated by Herbert Minton to All Saints, Church Leigh, Staffordshire, in 1851. The tiles bear the arms of Richard Bagot of Blithfield, who paid for the rebuilding of the church.

Encaustic memorial tile in the chancel of Holy Trinity church, Hartshill, Stoke-on-Trent, dedicated to Herbert Minton, who paid for the building of the church in 1842 and was buried there in 1858.

An early Minton & Company tile on the floor at Holy Trinity church, Hartshill, Stoke-on-Trent, depicting the Holy Ghost in the guise of a dove, 1842.

Minton & Company tiles on the floor of Salisbury Cathedral chapter house, based on medieval examples, c.1855.

Minton & Company tiles on the floor at Ely Cathedral, Cambridgeshire. The yellow enamel covering the buff-coloured inlay has for the most part worn off.

Minton & Company tiles on the steps of the choir at Great Malvern Priory, Worcestershire, based on medieval examples found in the church. The inlay has been painted with yellow enamel glaze, which has been well preserved on the tiles covering the wall and the risers of the steps.

Some of the earliest designs based on medieval patterns were used throughout the whole period; there was an influx of new ones about 1860 along with amplified manufacturing facilities. A standard, deeply imprinted back mark MINTON & CO PATENT STOKE UPON TRENT was used throughout the whole manufacturing period. Minton's 6 inch (152 mm) floor tiles were always made of plastic clay. About 1860 a smaller tile, 4¹/₄ inches (108 mm) square and proportionally thinner, came to be preferred by architects. Most are stamped MINTON HOLLINS & CO, the firm's new name, and some were produced by the pressed-dust process. On those tiles the name is in relief. The 6 inch (152 mm) square by 1 inch (25 mm) thick size continued to be made until the end of the century, though after 1860 they could be ordered in a ¹/₂ inch (12 mm) thickness. To churches ordering a floor of his tiles Minton would very often make a gift of the tiles east of the communion rail, and those were of the best sort. This show of genuine religious feeling cost the firm much profit; yet loss was somewhat balanced by the fact that, until after Herbert Minton's death in 1858, the firm seems to have had a virtual monopoly of the market, since no other make of tile is found among the many churches which used tiles in one area surveyed, the East Riding of Yorkshire.

GODWIN

This firm was founded in 1852 by William Godwin, a brickmaker of Lugwardine, Herefordshire, who was aided on the technical side by his brother Henry, who had had two years' experience of making inlaid tiles at the Maw factory at Worcester. At first their tiles had no distinguishing features: they were made in two finishes, either entirely unglazed or with a highly glazed, smooth surface like those of Chamberlain, whose tiles Godwin would have been familiar with at Worcester. The firm was in full production by 1853 when it was visited by the

Inlaid and line-impressed Godwin tiles at St Cuthbert, Durwen, Lancashire, c.1870.

Godwin tiles around the altar at Holy Trinity, Hull, c.1870.

Reverend E. L. Cutts, who was writing a book on *Church Furniture and Decoration.* He singled out for praise a tile of modern design, which implies that a departure from medieval style was at that time exceptional. In 1857 the firm received a prestigious order for tiles to pave the eastern part of Hereford Cathedral. This is still in fair condition and presents a most impressive display of Godwin's work. Random indentations on the tile surfaces gave an antique look which blended with the medieval surroundings, and this effect, with the size of $4^1/4$ inches (108 mm) square, which was nearer to the old dimension, at once commended them to ecclesiologists. By 1860 the randomly dented surface had standardised to a texture like orange peel, which henceforth was the standard finish and makes Godwin's tiles easily identifiable. Gilbert Scott and G. E. Street especially favoured Godwin tiles.

A large variety of back markings was used. An elaborate stamp was soon superseded by two

Below: Godwin tile with an image of the Virgin Mary, c.1870.

19

1830 SAMUEL WRIGHT of Shelton, Stoke, takes out patent for making inlaid tiles.

c.1835 Disposes of equipment and unsold stock to Herbert Minton and negotiates royalty agreement with him and also with Walter Chamberlain trading as CHAMBERLAIN & CO. of Worcester (c.1836).

1840 Minton starts successful manufacturing as MINTON & CO. of Stoke-on-Trent.

1840 Chamberlain amalga[mates] with Flight, Barr & Barr. China production concen[trated] at Chamberlain's works; t[...] to Flight, Barr & Barr, wh[...] George Barr and Fleming [...] take over.

1844 Wright gets seven-year patent extension and sells it outright, half to Minton, half to Chamberlain.

1845 Michael Daintry Hollins becomes a partner in Minton & Co. and takes charge of encaustic tile production. Style of firm changed to MINTON, HOLLINS & CO.

1850 Bought by John Horr[...] for his sons, who begin tra[...] MAW & CO.

1852 Maw & Co. moves fr[om...] to Benthall in Shropshire.

1849 Colin Minton Campbell becomes a partner in charge of china production.

1858 Herbert Minton dies.

1859 China works under Colin Minton Campbell and tile works under M. D. Hollins split into independent companies.

1863 Robert Minton Taylor made a partner.

Workmen le[...] of plain qua[...] valley to tur[...] BROSELEY [...] & CRAVEN [...] developing i[...] which, in a [...] considerabl[...]

1868 Name changed to Minton's China Works. It develops a great range of printed tiles.

1868 R. M. Taylor, M. D. Hollins and C. M. Campbell partnership dissolved.

1869 R. M. Taylor starts own factory at Fenton under style ROBERT MINTON TAYLOR.

1869 M. D. Hollins builds large new factory at Stoke. He is now sole proprietor of Minton, Hollins & Co.

1875 Colin Minton Campbell buys R. M. Taylor's tile works as a private venture. Name changed to THE CAMPBELL BRICK & TILE CO. Taylor stays on as manager. They move to Stoke in 1876.

1883 Maw builds a new fa[ctory...] Jackfield and continues to [...] throughout the century.

1882 Name changed to THE CAMPBELL TILE CO.

1962 Absorbed by H. & R. Johnson-Richards.

1968 Absorbed by Royal Doulton Tableware Group.

1968 Absorbed by H. & R. Johnson-Richards Tiles Ltd.

1969 Absorbed by H. & R. Johnson-Richards.

H. & R. Johnson-Richards Tiles Ltd of Stoke-on-Trent.

ARCHITECTURAL POTTERY CO., Poole, Dorset.
Founded in 1854 relying on technical help from John Ridgway of Hanley (possibly having worked at Minton). Its tiles, with an off-white clay body, are entirely unlike the tiles of any other company.

1861 Its manager, Walker, leaves to start T. W. WALKER'S PATENT ENCAUSTIC AND MOSAIC ORNAMENTAL BRICK & TILES MANUFACTORY.

1873 Jesse Carter buys out Walker.

ed

ester

1852 Henry Godwin leaves Maw and joins his brother William, who starts new company, WILLIAM GODWIN of Lugwardine, Hereford.

1876 Henry leaves to form own company.

aw enable makers
in the Severn
id church tiles.
ES and HARGREAVES
, the latter
VEN DUNNILL & CO.,
ory opened in 1875, achieved
s. Closed down 1951.

WORCESTER ST GEORGE'S ENCAUSTIC TILE CO. The St George's Pottery Works began to make church tiles about 1878. Its tiles much resemble Craven Dunnill's.

1880 Jesse Carter buys out the St George's Encaustic Tile Co.

Builds new factory, 'The Victoria Tile Works'.

1880 William's son, William Henry, joins company.

1883 Renamed GODWIN & SON.

1895 Jesse Carter buys the Architectural Pottery Co. and changes name to Carter's Tiles, Poole. Manufacture of encaustic tiles abandoned.

1884 Takes into partnership William Hewitt and changes name to GODWIN & HEWITT.

1906 Sold to a partnership making fireplace tiles. Encaustics abandoned.

1907 In liquidation. Sold to a partnership which ceases to manufacture encaustics.

1986 Shaw Hereford Tiles Ltd, the successor of both firms, continues to manufacture plain and decorated wall tiles up to the late 1980s.

Active tile production continued at Poole until the mid 1990s.

A selection of 4¼ inch (108 mm) tiles (post-1860). Rows 1 and 2, Maw & Company; rows 3, 4, 5, 6, Godwin; rows 7, 8, 9, Minton & Company (Minton Hollins).

Above. *An unusual arrangement of Maw & Company tiles in the shape of a coffin at Battlefield church near Shrewsbury, 1862.*

Below: *A simple but striking arrangement of Maw & Company tiles in the sanctuary of St Mary's parish church, Princes Risborough, Buckinghamshire, 1868.*

lines of type: WM. GODWIN, LUGWARDINE (a style Godwin would have seen on Chamberlain's tiles at Worcester). When dust-pressing had been adopted, it was changed to relief lettering between raised bands. Finally came various 'target' patterns (concentric circles) with raised lettering, with more than forty variants in all.

MAW & COMPANY

John Hornby Maw made his fortune as a manufacturing chemist in London, selling out at the age of thirty-four. He retired to Brighton, then moved to Worcester in the 1840s, where he began collecting tracings of medieval tiles as a hobby. Of his two sons, George and Arthur, the first shared his father's technical and antiquarian interests. When it was known that Chamberlain were giving up their tilemaking department, J. H. Maw decided to buy. Designs, moulds

Maw & Company tiles in the spandrels of the arches in the chapel of St James's Hospital, Leeds, 1861.

and stock were taken over and the Maws, no doubt employing some of Chamberlain's workmen, began manufacturing church tiles in 1850. Father and two sons made a well-qualified management team and the firm went on to become serious competitors to Minton & Company.

In 1852 they moved higher up the Severn to Benthall, to a site better suited to the expansion they planned. Although the address stamped on their tiles was 'Benthall Works, Broseley', 'near Broseley' would have been more accurate. When the firm moved again in 1883, to Jackfield nearby, the name 'Benthall Works' was retained.

For the first ten years Maw & Company confined their production to church tiles and it was not until the 1860s that they began to make wall tiles in great variety and patent tiles to imitate tessellated mosaic. Maw's first catalogue of church tiles was issued in 1853 and contained some 160 designs made up of some of Chamberlain's patterns, several copied from the newly published first part of *Specimens of Tile Pavements* by Henry Shaw and the remainder presumably from tracings made by J. H. or George Maw from medieval originals. In general Maw favoured more complicated patterns than other makers and by 1890 had introduced into their range of church tiles many designs by J. P. Seddon and George Goldie which showed only a slight trace of traditional Gothic.

Twenty-four 6 inch (152 mm) tiles by Maw & Company. The top three rows are from their 1853 catalogue; the four designs in the first row were taken over from Chamberlain & Company; rows 4 and 5 are from the firm's 1862 catalogue; the bottom row from their catalogue of about 1900.

Maw's first markings on the backs of their tiles, before the move to Benthall, acknowledged the firm's origin by introducing the letters CW for Chamberlain of Worcester. Their first Broseley mark was also an all-over design. They next adopted a treatment copied from Minton's – twenty-five stabbed holes with MAW & CO BENTHALL WORKS BROSELEY SALOP deeply imprinted in large letters with the addition of the workman's number. When dust-pressing was adopted, their mark took the form of raised bars with relief letters between.

ROBERT MINTON TAYLOR

R. M. Taylor, a nephew of Herbert Minton, became a partner in the tilemaking firm of Minton, Hollins & Company in 1863. The partnership was dissolved in 1869 when Taylor started his own factory at Fenton, Stoke-on-Trent. Using the talents of good designers, he had considerable success with some distinguished pavements, finding patrons mainly in neighbouring counties. From the start he used variously coloured clays for inlay and also developed a range of subjects in matching styles such as 'Instruments of the Passion', 'The Evangelists' and other Christian symbols. His mark, impressed, was ROBERT MINTON TAYLOR TILE WORKS FENTON NEAR STOKE-ON-TRENT. His tile fabric is usually 'sandwich' (coarser clay between thin layers of finer clay) and $1/2$ inch (12 mm) thick. The company was bought by Colin Minton Campbell in 1875.

25

THE CAMPBELL BRICK & TILE COMPANY

Colin Minton Campbell, another nephew of Herbert Minton, was in charge of the china side of the business from 1849 and greatly expanded production of printed wall tiles, which were back-stamped MINTONS CHINA WORKS. Clearly his interest inclined strongly to tiles, for when his cousin Robert Minton Taylor was looking for capital to realise the full potential of his own floor tile business Campbell offered to buy the concern, retaining Robert as manager. A new company was launched in 1875 as the Minton Brick & Tile Company but when the name was disallowed by a court case it was changed to the Campbell Brick & Tile Company. In 1876 they moved to a new factory at Stoke.

Encaustic tile with the head of the apostle Judas, who committed suicide by hanging; Campbell Brick & Tile Company, c.1880.

R. M. Taylor had accumulated a large repertory of moulds which Campbell had little need to enlarge, as church building was passing its peak. Subsequent tile production is, therefore, hardly to be distinguished from that of the former owner. A fairly sure indication of make, however, is the date when tiles were laid. Some of the moulds made for inlaid tiles were equally suitable for the coloured enamels used to obtain the majolica effect, and some notable successes were achieved under the new owner, of which the cover illustration is an example.

Campbell's tiles are generally 6 inches (152 mm) square by $^1/_2$ inch (12 mm) thick. Like R. M. Taylor's tiles, most are of 'sandwich' construction with stabbed holes. Their mark is a device showing the four points of the compass encircled by the firm's name THE CAMPBELL BRICK & TILE COMPANY. By this time many church tiles were being glazed and Campbell followed the fashion. He also adopted the dust-pressed method and made no attempt to imitate a medieval surface

Rows 1, 2, 3, Robert Minton Taylor/Campbell Brick & Tile Company; rows 4, 5, 6, 7, Craven Dunnill & Company.

finish. Mosaic of variously shaped plain tiles was a speciality of this company.

CRAVEN DUNNILL & COMPANY

This firm was the last of several makers of encaustic tiles to be established in the Severn valley. It grew out of the partnership of Hawes and Denny, active in the 1860s. Hawes dropped out and Hargreaves and Craven entered the firm and traded under that name. Then Hargreaves and Denny left and Craven took into partnership their former manager H. P. Dunnill. As the businessman, Dunnill brought in shareholders and this enabled the firm to build a fine new factory in 1875 at Jackfield, close to that of Maw & Company.

Craven Dunnill's inlaid tiles were made from plastic clay and for the first few years can be distinguished only by their moulds. After 1880, however, they began to aim, very successfully, at an authentic medieval look, reproducing, in addition to a lumpy surface, slight deviations from perfect symmetry. These later tiles are glazed, producing a deep yellow colour over the inlay. Another speciality, practised only rarely by other makers (such

Far left: *An encaustic tile showing a design of medieval dragons, Craven Dunnill, c.1880. The imperfections in the surface are an attempt to create an authentic medieval look.*

Left: *Encaustic church tile covered with a thick honey-coloured glaze, Craven Dunnill, c.1880.*

as Godwins), was the production of tiles with line-impressed decoration with all-over green, yellow or brown glaze, pooled in the hollows, reproducing closely a group of medieval tiles found in Ireland and in Cheshire. Some of their tiles of about 1885 show wholly original designs which hardly connect with their own or any other period.

Back markings took the form of five raised bars and, in raised lettering, CRAVEN DUNNILL & CO JACKFIELD. Although at first glance these tiles look dust-pressed, there are indications such as fingerprints in the clay or warping of the body which prove otherwise. It was probably realised that dust-pressing did not achieve anything like a medieval look.

OTHER MAKERS

In addition to the firms already mentioned, church tiles were made by: the Architectural Pottery Company of Poole; Broseley Tileries; J. C. Edwards, Ruabon; Thorn, Broseley; St George's Worcester Encaustic Tile Company; W. Whetstone, Coalville; Martyn White, Gresley; and Wedgwood of Etruria.

Above: *Craven Dunnill relief tiles on the floor of Bangor Cathedral, Gwynedd, put in during the restoration by Sir Gilbert Scott c.1875.*

Right: *Craven Dunnill line-impressed tiles on the floor of Bangor Cathedral, c.1875. They are probably based on line-impressed medieval tiles found at the cathedral.*

28

Encaustic church tile based on a medieval design made by the Architectural Pottery Company, Poole, c.1875.

Glazed encaustic tiles for domestic hearths and corridors were made by a dozen or so other manufacturers.

While manufacturers were including encaustic tiles in their lists as late as 1920, they are seldom seen in a church built in the twentieth century. Inescapable hand processes were making inlaid tiles unduly expensive, added to which fashions had changed. The preference for plain floors by at least one influential church architect, Temple Moore (1856–1920), accelerated the trend. His style was characterised by strength and simplicity and decorated tiles had no place. Henceforth floors were of stone, marble or plain tiles. As had happened at the close of the Middle Ages, at the end of the nineteenth century the use of inlaid floor tiles in churches ceased.

Above: *Encaustic floor tiles at St John the Evangelist, Rhosymedre, in North Wales, attributed to the firm of J. C. Edwards in nearby Ruabon, 1887–8. The panels depict Christ in the guise of a Holy Lamb.*

Occasionally nineteenth-century encaustic church tiles were imported from abroad, as can be seen in the mortuary chapel of Napoleon III, built in 1874 at St Mary's church, Chislehurst, Kent. The tiles were made by the French firm Boulenger at Auneuil, near Beauvais. The floor tiles show the emblems of Napoleon III.

A 6 inch (152 mm) Minton & Company encaustic tile designed by A. W. N. Pugin to display his monogram, probably for his own house, The Grange at Ramsgate, 1843–4.

Both of Samuel Wright's original licensees were in touch with architects of Gothic persuasion. Minton had met Pugin before 1840, probably when Pugin was employed at Alton Towers. Chamberlain was well acquainted with Harvey Eginton (1809–49), County Surveyor of Worcestershire, and was also helped by Thomas Willement, the glass-painter.

When compiling his first catalogue in 1842, Minton was given a good start with the Westminster Abbey floor-tile designs he had been called on to reproduce. Other designs were culled from the medieval patterns in Parker's *Glossary of Architecture* (1840 edition) and from the first part of J. G. Nichols's *Examples* (1841). From the early 1840s to about 1850 Pugin designed scores of original patterns for the Palace of Westminster, all of which appeared on tiles made by Minton. Since architects specified the manufacturer it was natural that tilemakers should apply to architects for new designs, and when an architect wished to pave a church with replicas of the medieval tiles found in it he sent specimens of the old tiles with his order. This was quite a common procedure in the southern counties. As the illustrations show, all the earlier manufacturers went to the same published sources for some of their medieval designs.

George Gilbert Scott (1811–78) was much impressed by the uniformity and surface finish of Godwin's work and 'invariably specified Mr Godwin's tiles' (*Building News,* 1890). G. E. Street (1824–81) was also an admirer of Godwin's tiles. When the need arose for an armorial shield or monogram the architect's office would provide a tracing. Maw & Company used the design services of M. Digby Wyatt (1820–77), Owen Jones (1809–74), G.

Minton & Company tiles designed by A. W. N. Pugin on the floor of St Nicholas's church, Peper Harow, Shackleford, Surrey, late 1840s. The tiles in the centre bear the arms of Lord Midleton and are surrounded by tiles with the M of the Virgin Mary. Tiles showing the emblems of the four Evangelists have been placed at the corners.

Maw & Company tiles in the Lady Chapel, Chester Cathedral, c.1880. The original design by George Goldie is preserved at Clive House Museum, Shrewsbury.

E. Street, J. P. Seddon (1827–1906) and George Goldie (1828–87). Robert Minton Taylor also benefited from the considerable ability of J. P. Seddon. Craven Dunnill had designs from George Goldie, J. F. Bentley (1839–1902) and Alfred Waterhouse (1830–1905).

Thus architects were often involved with the designs of individual tiles. Some drawings by Street showing whole pavements for his churches, preserved in the RIBA library, indicate that, whereas the position of panels, runners, borders and so on were his concern, the choice of individual tile designs in these cases was left to others.

ARRANGEMENTS

The decorative effect of any pavement using ornamented tiles relies very much on their arrangement: light against dark, decorated tiles beside plain ones. The idea that hundreds of patterned tiles *en bloc* were beautiful in proportion to their number (there is an example of about 1843 in St Mary's, Stafford) was soon corrected by a closer study of medieval work, the basic arrangement of which was a criss-cross of plain bands enclosing groups of four, nine or sixteen decorated tiles. Such a scheme also reduced the number of expensive inlaid tiles required.

A lithographic print showing an arrangement of Minton & Company tiles in the shape of a cross. It was found in the scrapbook of a nineteenth-century architect and probably dates from the early 1840s.

Top: *Page from a catalogue of the firm of Francis Morton, engineers and contractors of iron churches in Liverpool, c.1870. It shows encaustic tile arrangements by Maw & Company for use in churches.*

Top middle: *An encaustic tile pavement with an exhortation to pray, on the floor of St Giles's church, Cheadle, Staffordshire. Minton & Company and other manufacturers made encaustic tiles with single letters that could be assembled to form inscriptions.*

Bottom middle: *Circular tile pavement made by Godwin in the sanctuary of Bishop Wilton church, North Yorkshire, built by the architect J. L. Pearson in 1858–9. The pavement seems to have been inspired by the medieval circular pavements with inlaid mosaic tiles found at Jervaulx Abbey.*

Bottom: *Minton & Company tiles on the floor at Lichfield Cathedral. The central tiles show a scene from the Old Testament in which Moses strikes a rock to find water, thus saving the Jews wandering through the desert from death by dehydration. Subsidiary scenes related to the central narrative are depicted on circular tiles in the four corners, c.1860.*

The inventive Victorians showed much ingenuity in their tile arrangements and the later manufacturers' catalogues give more space to this aspect than to individual tile patterns. They offered to devise schemes for any patron who sent in the precise dimensions and shape of the area to be covered. Arrangements favoured in different decades are sometimes a better guide to the dating of a floor than looking at individual tiles, since makers did not jettison moulds so long as they were in demand. Border tiles fulfilled a practical function. When the tiles were being laid, boards were laid around the edge, upon which a wooden 'straight edge' could be rested, ensuring flatness for the whole surface. The edging boards were finally lifted and tiles of the same width dropped into place.

The best nineteenth-century tiled floors are to be seen in cathedrals and usually formed part of an extensive restoration. Paradoxically, however, they are not the easiest to identify

Right: A circular Minton & Company tile on the floor of Lichfield Cathedral. It relates to an Old Testament scene showing the Sacrifice of Isaac and depicts a ram, which was sacrificed by Abraham in the place of his son Isaac. The design and execution of the tile are of the highest quality and craftsmanship.

Below: A circular encaustic tile made by Minton & Company depicting the evangelist St Luke in the guise of a winged ox set within an elaborate border design, c.1860. It is before the altar at Holy Trinity church, Skipton, North Yorkshire.

because familiar designs may be absent, as new sets of moulds, special to the contracts, were perhaps deemed more appropriate. The tiled area sometimes extended from the choir screen to the reredos and could measure 100 feet (30 metres) long by 30 feet (9 metres) wide. Tremendous effort went into the work since it attracted much notice and formed a permanent show of the firm's finest wares. Minton and Godwin each claimed to have made pavements for nine cathedrals. Maw did little work in this field in England and the only other cathedral tiles the writers have seen have been by Craven Dunnill at Bangor, Chester and Kirkwall.

A mosaic floor of rectangles, hexagons, triangles or rhombi without any inlaid tiles is not unusual in country churches. Intended for corridors in houses, this kind of floor was, no doubt, laid for economic reasons. Several makers produced them.

Below: An encaustic commemorative tile made by Minton & Company and dedicated to John Lonsdale, Bishop of Lichfield, in the sanctuary of St Mark's church, Shelton, Stoke-on-Trent, 1867.

WALL TILES

In Stoke-on-Trent and other centres of manufacture, where it was easy to obtain tiles with custom-made designs, wall monuments made of inlaid inscribed tiles were popular. An extensive series may be seen in the church of St Peter ad Vincula, Stoke, and also in Minton's own church of Holy Trinity, Hartshill. Floor tiles are not infrequently seen

Encaustic tiles designed by A. W. N. Pugin and made by Minton & Company, in front of the altar at St Mark's church, Shelton, Stoke-on-Trent.

A floor arrangement of Minton & Company tiles at St Albans Cathedral as part of the restoration devised and paid for by Lord Grimthorpe about 1885. Many of the tiles are copies of the medieval ones found during the work.

Two encaustic Minton & Company tiles with heraldic lions at St Albans Cathedral, c.1885.

on interior walls, but the best kind of wall tiling has relief decoration glazed with majolica enamels. Minton and Maw favoured Moorish designs while the Campbell Brick & Tile Company carried out some ambitious schemes in the Neo-Gothic style, as seen on the front cover.

Another dimension to the subject of nineteenth-century church tiles is large hand-painted wall panels produced specifically for ecclesiastical interiors. A well-known example is William Butterfield's All Saints' Church, Margaret Street, London. Here one can find not only Minton tiles on the floor, but also large tile panels on the walls showing saints designed by Butterfield, painted on the tiles by Alexander Gibbs and fired by Henry Poole & Sons. Other firms such as Morris & Company, W. B. Simpson & Sons and Doulton & Company also undertook commissions for churches. Morris & Company

Above left. *Painted wall tiles surrounding the tomb of Bishop Selwyn at Lichfield Cathedral, c.1878. They show scenes and emblematic devices relating to his missionary work in New Zealand.*

Above right: *Detail of a tiled reredos showing two archangels at Clapham church, Sussex, made by Morris & Company, 1873–4.*

made wall tiles showing minstrel angels at Findon church, Sussex, in 1867–8. More Morris & Company examples can be seen at Clapham church, also in Sussex, which has a painted reredos depicting the four archangels installed in 1873–4. In the same church there are also painted panels flanking the chancel windows, depicting the apostles and made by W. B. Simpson & Sons. A tiled commemorative plaque with an angel in red by Doulton in memory of Eby Gray, who died in 1892 aged twenty-nine, can still be admired in the parish church of Parton near Castle Douglas in Scotland.

Glazed encaustic tiles with the IHS monogram set amongst majolica tiles on the wall of the sanctuary of St John the Evangelist, Rhosymedre, Wrexham, Wales. It is part of an elaborately tiled reredos made by the workers of the firm of J. C. Edwards in nearby Ruabon in 1906, in remembrance of their employer J. C. Edwards.

Identification and dating

Once a tile has been identified it may generally be assumed that all other tiles in that area of floor are by the same maker. If a church was built before 1851 and has not been restored or beautified, then any nineteenth-century tiles are by Minton or Chamberlain. Chamberlain's tiles are glazed, Minton's of similar date are either entirely unglazed or with yellow enamel covering the pattern only. Occasionally they are glazed all over, especially when used on walls. A glazed surface with an even 'orange peel' texture is by Godwin. Tiles with lumpy surfaces, imparting a medieval look, are likely to be by Craven Dunnill, Carter & Company (St George's Tile Works, Worcester) or by J. C. Edwards of Ruabon.

Certain designs were adopted by almost all makers, for example, the fleur-de-lis. Though it is the symbol of the Virgin, its decorative value could not be ignored and it was widely used in Protestant churches.

Because of a time span of only sixty years moulds made when production began were still in use at the end, so other clues are needed. Pavements laid before 1845 tend to be composed entirely of decorated tiles. Before 1855 nearly all tiles were 6 inches (152 mm) square. After that $4^1/4$ inches (108 mm) square is more usual. Tiles entirely without glaze tend to date from about 1842–70. Inlaid tiles in a Neo-Gothic church built before 1836 must have been

Left: *The back of a Minton & Company tile showing the name of the manufacturer and the place of manufacture. It also shows two date marks indicating the year (a diamond with a cross on top for 1862) and the month (the letter D for December) in which the tile was made.*

Below: *The backs of two encaustic tiles. Left: A tile made from malleable clay with stab marks and impressed letters reading* MAW & CO BENTHALL BROSELEY. *Right: A tile made from dust-pressed clay with raised letters reading* W GODWIN LUGWARDINE HEREFORD.

Six fleur-de-lis tiles made by various manufacturers. (Top row, left to right) Maw & Company, Minton & Company, Thorn. (Bottom row, left to right) Broseley Tile Company, Godwin, Robert Minton Taylor.

added at a later date. A church built after 1841 will have tiles of the same date as the building unless there were later alterations. Nineteenth-century tiles in a medieval church usually date from a restoration, the date of which can generally be learned from a guide-book. The arrangement of the tiles in a pavement also provides clues.

The best way of acquiring examples of church tiles is to be on the spot during a demolition. One church will contain many more tiles than the antique trade can take, so the surplus is usually dumped. There is, as yet, little appreciation of their technical excellence, their inherent historical interest or schematic qualities and they are seldom found in antique shops or fairs. However, the pace of demolition is slowing and it will not be long before remaining pavements of inlaid tiles are prized and carefully guarded. Some specialist dealers in London often have encaustic tiles in stock.

In Britain there is no special club of church tile collectors, but the Tiles and Architectural Ceramics Society has a nationwide membership among which there are many members who collect and study church tiles. If you would like more information, write to the Secretary, Myra Brown, Decorative Arts Department, Liverpool Museum, William Brown Street, Liverpool L3 8EN.

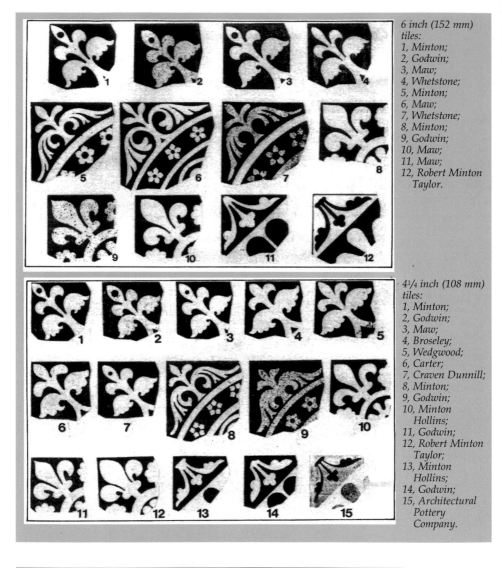

6 inch (152 mm) tiles:
1, Minton;
2, Godwin;
3, Maw;
4, Whetstone;
5, Minton;
6, Maw;
7, Whetstone;
8, Minton;
9, Godwin;
10, Maw;
11, Maw;
12, Robert Minton Taylor.

4¼ inch (108 mm) tiles:
1, Minton;
2, Godwin;
3, Maw;
4, Broseley;
5, Wedgwood;
6, Carter;
7, Craven Dunnill;
8, Minton;
9, Godwin;
10, Minton Hollins;
11, Godwin;
12, Robert Minton Taylor;
13, Minton Hollins;
14, Godwin;
15, Architectural Pottery Company.

Complete tiles. The makers of these four tiles may be identified by comparison with the corner details shown above.

Further reading

MEDIEVAL TILES
Eames, Elizabeth. *English Tilers*. British Museum Publications Ltd, 1992.
Lemmen, H. van. *Medieval Tiles*. Shire, 2000.

NINETEENTH-CENTURY TILES
Austwick, J. and B. *The Decorated Tile*. Pitman, 1980.
Barnard, Julian. *Victorian Ceramic Tiles*. Studio Vista, 1972.
Herbert, T., and Huggins, K. *The Decorative Tile*. Phaidon, 1995.
Jewitt, Llewellyn. *The Ceramic Art of Great Britain*. First edition, 1878; facsimile reprint 1971.
Lemmen, H. van. *Victorian Tiles*. Shire, second edition 2000.
Messenger, Michael. *Pottery and Tiles of the Severn Valley*. Remploy, 1979.
Skinner, D., and Lemmen, H. van. *Minton Tiles 1835–1935*. City Museum and Art Gallery, Stoke-on-Trent, 1984.

The Tiles and Architectural Ceramics Society website, with information on the locations of church tiles, is at www.tilesoc.org.uk

Places to visit

More than half the churches in Britain made use of decorated floor tiles and there are also some churches with decorative and pictorial wall tiles. The following is a selection of some with a better than average display or of particular interest. The names of churches are inserted only when there is more than one church in a place. The dates are tentative, being either the building of the church, its restoration, or sometimes, in the case of Minton, the date of the donation of tiles. When makers are known, they are indicated thus: BT, Broseley Tileries; D, Doulton; C, Chamberlain; CB, Campbell Brick & Tile Company; CD, Craven Dunnill; G, Godwin; JCE, J. C. Edwards; M, Minton/Minton Hollins; MW, Maw; RMT, Robert Minton Taylor; WM, William Morris; WBS, W. B. Simpson & Sons.

Buckinghamshire
Princes Risborough, St Mary (MW, 1868).

Cambridgeshire
Ely Cathedral (M); Sawtry (MW); Sutton (M, c.1843).

Cheshire
Chester Cathedral: Choir (CD), Lady Chapel (MW).

Cumbria
Carlisle Cathedral (G); Coniston (MW, 1891).

Derbyshire
Ashbourne (RMT); Derby, St Mary (M, c.1860).

Devon
Buckland Monachorum (MW); Exeter Cathedral (G).

Dorset
Christchurch Priory (G); Wimborne Minster (M, 1857).

Gloucestershire
Cheltenham (G); Cirencester (G); Gloucester Cathedral (M, G); Highnam (G); Tewkesbury Abbey (G).

Hampshire
Winchester, St Cross (M).

Herefordshire
Hereford Cathedral (G, 1857); Lugwardine (G).

Hertfordshire
St Albans Abbey (M, c.1885).

Kent
Chislehurst, St Mary (tiles by Boulenger, Auneuil, France, 1874); Rochester Cathedral (G); Ramsgate, St Augustine (M, c.1848).

Lancashire
Darwen, St Cuthbert (G).

Lincolnshire
Bigby (M); Lincoln Cathedral (M, 1857–8); Louth, St James: Sanctuary (M), south porch (MW).

London
All Saints, Margaret Street (M and wall tiles designed by Butterfield); Temple Church (M,

1842); Herne Hill, St Paul (M).

Shropshire
Jackfield (MW, 1863); Kemberton (CD, 1882); Shrewsbury, Battlefield (M, MW, 1862); Shrewsbury, St Mary (M, MW and G).

Somerset
Bath, St John (M, 1863); Wells Cathedral (M).

Staffordshire
Brewood (M, 1856); Burslem, St John (CB, c.1880); Cheadle, St Giles (M, 1846); Church Leigh (M, 1845 and 1851); Enville (M, 1875); Lichfield Cathedral (M, c.1860); Newcastle-under-Lyme, St George (M, 1854); Stafford, St Mary (M, 1844); Stoke-on-Trent, Penkhull, St Thomas (M, 1845); Stoke-on-Trent, Shelton, St Mark (M, 1866); Stoke-on-Trent, Stoke, St Peter ad Vincula (M); Stoke-on-Trent, Hartshill, Holy Trinity (M, 1842; RMT, 1872); Trentham (M, 1844 and 1870); Tunstall, Christ Church (CB, 1885).

Surrey
Albury Old Church (M, 1842); Redhill (C, 1843); Godalming, St Peter and St Paul (G); Peper Harow, St Nicholas (M, c.1848).

Sussex
Findon (WM, 1867–8); Clapham (WM and WBS, 1873–4).

West Midlands
Oscott, St Mary's College (M, c.1860).

Wiltshire
Devizes, St John (1875); East Grafton (C); Salisbury Cathedral, chapter house (M, c.1855).

Worcestershire
Great Malvern Priory (M, G, C); Sedgeberrow (G, 1868); Worcester Cathedral (G).

East Yorkshire
Anlaby (CD, 1885); Barmby Moor (M, 1849 and 1851); Beswick (M, 1871); Beverley, St Mary (G, 1867); Bishop Wilton (G, 1860); Hedon (M, 1844); Hull, Holy Trinity (G, 1870); Newport (G, 1898); Pocklington (CB, 1885); Rise (M, 1843); Scorborough (M, 1859); South Dalton (MW, 1861); Yapham (M).

North Yorkshire
Baldersby (1858); Boroughbridge (M, 1852); Coverham (MW, majolica); Hunmanby (BT); Kirby Grindalythe (G, 1878); Knapton (MW, 1871); Masham (G); Newton-on-Ouse (M, 1848); Scampston (M, 1842); Skipton, Holy Trinity (M); Thorpe Bassett (CD, 1880); Weaverthorpe (G, 1872); Welburn (M, 1865); Wheldrake (RMT, 1875); Willerby (CD, 1882); York, Minster chapter house (M, 1845); York, Saints Philip and James (M, 1867).

South Yorkshire
Doncaster, Christ Church (M).

West Yorkshire
Bradford, St James (WBS); Harewood (M); Leeds, Parish Church (G, c.1875); Leeds, St James's Hospital Chapel (MW, 1861); Leeds, Woodhouse, St Mark (CB); Leeds, Headingley, St Michael and All Angels (G, c.1875); Weeton (M, 1851–3).

Wales
Bangor Cathedral (CD, 1876); Haverfordwest, Slebech church (C); Knighton (M, 1877); Leighton (M, 1853); St Asaph Cathedral (MW, c.1870); St David's Cathedral (G); Old Radnor parish church (G); Rhosymedre, St John the Evangelist (JCE, 1887 and 1906); Welshpool (G).

Scotland
Castle Douglas, Parton parish church (D); Edinburgh, St Giles (G); Kirkwall, St Magnus Cathedral (CD).

Craven Dunnill tiles in the choir of Chester Cathedral, c.1880.